I0149168

All Scripture references taken from the KJV of the Bible unless otherwise indicated.

Too Many Women: Wonder Why You Have Lady Problems

www.marlenemilestheauthor.com

Freshwater Press, USA

freshwaterpress9@gmail.com

ISBN: 978-1-960150-52-3

Table of Contents

Too Many Wives

Wonder Why You Have Lady Problems

Freshwater

Freshwater Press, USA

Polygamy

Looking at the word, *polygamy* my first thought is that this has nothing to do with me. I do not have multiple husbands and would never be a sister-wife.

But--, is that what all the talk in the NT was about such as Deacons being the husband of one wife and such--, *polygamy*? In the OT those OG's had multiple wives, handmaidens, and concubines, it was too much, really. Surely, they used the *Be fruitful and multiply* clause from Genesis to award themselves the indulgence of *whoredoms*.

Okay, so this really has nothing to do with me. My mother was married only to my father, even from a young age. My dad only wedded my mother, all of us kids have the same mom and dad, who came home by dinnertime every night. This polygamy talk must be about Mormons, OT people, and kings with concubines. There are religions that still allow men to load up on wives, even today. Some Islamic, Hindu countries, Native American, Indigenous Australian, and Mongolian people practice *group marriage*, which is having multiple husbands and multiple wives. Else and elsewhere, polygamy is prohibited so there's no way my parents would be bigamists or polygamists.

No way ---, until I listened to a teaching on **polygamous witchcraft** by Dr. Daniel Olukoya who is a pastor and prayer general of the Lord. Find him on YouTube, for messages on this subject.

If you are affected by this, I am presupposing you want to be set free from the *spirit of polygamy*. If you don't know if it has anything to do with you yet, keep reading this book and find out exactly what it is and what it does to a family, a person, a child, a life.

The *spirit of polygamy* will have you behaving in a way that you may think is normal, but it is not because it is not of God. If it is what you saw from your childhood, growing up, you may think it's normal, but there is so much better for you and everyone that you deal with in life. Papa was a rolling stone, baby momma drama, serial cheating, and multiple divorces are not Godly models.

Those are satanic models, actually. People in the devil's system are remote controlled; they do what the devil instructs, influences, or programs them to do.

Polygamy, for instance, to the dominant spouse, is fun. It makes them feel important or powerful. To the victim-spouse it further victimizes them if they don't have confidence, self-esteem, a way out, or knowledge that they don't have to put up with sharing a spouse with another or others. They knowingly rob their children of a proper father and relegate them to a life of *less than.*

While Men Slept

*But while men slept, his enemy came and sowed
tares among the wheat, and went his way.*
(Matthew 13:25)

A lot of our problems come when we are
asleep because our spirit is awake while our
bodies are asleep. We make deals and can get
into evil spiritual covenants that can devastate
both our spiritual and natural lives. If the
memory of the *dream* is wiped, and that can
happen, we have no idea what we did for up to
a third of our Earth lives. If we live to be 100,
that's 30 years' worth of activities and deal
making in the night, in the spirit that we can't
account for. If we pay no attention to dreams,

that's 30 years of **living** that we are clueless about, but we are still responsible as if we did.

If the dreams are blanketed, we have no idea what we signed up for in our night escapades. Further, if our ancestors set us up with the *spirit of polygamy*, or worse, we don't know **what** they agreed to, either. How many of us know the ancestor who lived 235 years ago, or anything about him or her?

Exactly.

While men slept his enemies came and sowed tares (weeds). The majority of our trouble could come to us as we sleep. How do we defend ourselves against this?

Who am I kidding? Some people are asleep while they are awake. They are spiritually asleep, even in the daytime. Daily amusements make us all like dingbat Disney cartoon characters while witchcraft swirls around our heads like Cinderella's birds. We are amused to distraction, like watching spinning wheels and rolling dice in a casino. We must stay sober and prayerful to defend ourselves against falling into foolish traps and making evil covenants.

Getting married in the dream is a *spirit marriage*; now that person has a spirit spouse. If you have a spouse in the natural and also one in your dream life, then that is the *spirit of polygamy* working against you. Even if you're not married in the natural, the *spirit spouse* has to go!

This book, however, is more about multiple *spouses* **in the natural**, however. Polygamous witchcraft is the worst outcome of polygamy. **Polygamous witchcraft** is one of the most damning of all types of witchcraft.

Thou shalt not suffer a witch to live,

(Exodus 22:18).

We must walk over what God tells us to tread upon and not embrace it and try to live with it.

- Every serpent and scorpion assigned against my destiny; I trample it under the soles of my feet, like ashes, in the Name of Jesus.

In countries where women are oppressed, where they may not have civil, social, or political rights, they secretly fight back with *witchcraft*. This is **not** spiritually justified; their mistreatment does not make it right. A witch will still have to answer for their actions; they may become spiritually captive, and judged, even lose their life.

If you've made a funky devil deal and ended up in an evil contract, and therefore in CAPTIVITY, how do you think you'll get out of captivity? Jesus Christ. Amen.

If you don't have Jesus Christ, you may try to get out by hook or crook, *MacGyvering* your way out, or if desperation is reached --, a person may try witchcraft. Dark arts are a losing proposition because witchcraft gets one deeper into captivity. The witch has made a deal with Satan who then establishes an *internal* altar in that witch. Now, they are controlled in the natural **and** in the spirit--, call it remote control.

According to Exodus 22:13, our Christian duty is to kill witchcraft. The enemy holds onto any ground he gets, even if he stole it or tricked somebody to get it. Christians, even if we are feeling wrongfully oppressed, we don't co-mingle with witchcraft, and we have to fight against it when we encounter it. So says the Word of God. This takes spiritual warfare.

Some feel spiritual warfare is too much. The only way to solve spiritual problems is *spiritually*. Spiritual problems are solved with spiritual warfare. If you are *captive*, you need fire power to get away from guards and strongmen jailers. War is loud, violent and intense. When war has been declared on you, spiritual warfare is not *too much*.

If a person is fighting on one battlefront but he needs to be on four or five--, if multiple altars are working against him because he was oblivious for years while the witchcraft attacks compounded, this man may need to step up his spiritual warfare. When evil altars have been established against you; you will need spiritual support. Spiritual warfare invokes the angels of God and powerful weapons of His armory to fight all that is coming against you, either in strength, numbers, or both.

Dr. Olukoya says, *"The best way to escape a problem is to solve it."* I say, let's solve it down to the root. Let's uproot it, let's dismiss it; let's exile it. There. Now there is peace internally, and peace in the land.

To do this, use specific *types* of prayers. We can start with, *Lord help*, or prayers of thanksgiving, but we need spiritual warfare, prayers of decree and declaration. Fire prayers. Judgmental prayers. Atomic prayers. Dangerous prayers. Spiritual warfare is a prayer battle. I recommend the ***Whosoever* Prayer Battle** by Pastor Nnenna Oti-Akerele. Get your hands on her book to take the enemy out of your business and your life.

Spiritual Weapons

God puts many spiritual weapons at our disposal. One necessary weapon is spiritual discernment. If people cannot *see* the problem--, see what the problem is, they won't find the solution.

Further, what you don't **know**, you won't **see**. So, we have to study to show ourselves approved. We need the Word of God. We need the Spirit of God, and we need to know how to work our weapons of war.

The book, *Living for the NOW of God*, by this author goes deeply into building your spiritual warhead for spiritual warfare.

Polygamous Witchcraft

Polygamous witchcraft is an evil sequela of multiple wives and numerous children. Yet all these kids will be lackluster, average or even below-average. They may not be non-achievers, but they will appear to be held back developmentally. Their hold ups and delays will more than likely be because of *polygamous witchcraft.*

- Any power that wants me to suffer and struggle, be buried alive, in the Name of Jesus

God arises and the enemy scatters.

Powerful people can be brought down by polygamous witchcraft. Promising children can be derailed by it. Households can be destroyed by jealousy, bitterness, and competition. Peninnah tormented Hannah but not to the point of witchcraft; Hannah made the right decision and went to the temple and prayed to the Lord until He answered.

How many books and movies have starred the evil stepmother? The evil stepfather? When stepmothers go to war against one another things get ugly fast. Is it better for a stepmother to stay away from the ex-wife, or for them to make *fake* friends? Hmmm. When the stepmother wars against a stepchild it is foul since the child usually knows nothing about this type of war.

More than one woman in a household could very well be when the spiritual tampering or blind cursing of the children starts. It could be when the black arts are deployed against the current and/or other spouses.

Esau married two pagan wives. Pagan means, *not God* so you can guess what his household was like. God banned kings from having multiple wives.

Problems multiply with polygamy. David had a man killed to enter into polygamy. Solomon didn't listen.

Spiritual polygamy in your heart is still polygamy and you are liable for the consequences of "heart" sins. Water of polygamy is bitter. Having an official or *unofficial* husband or wife is still polygamy, even if you don't marry them "on paper." Men with multiple girlfriends, even if they are not simultaneous are still polygamous. Both men and women who think dating a thousand people is okay. God says it's not.

This is spiritual; you can't hide from it.

Any man with a strange woman that they are not legally married to is practicing polygamy. When a person cannot commit to one partner, that is the *spirit of polygamy.*

Dr. Anthony Akerele describes that the call of lust comes on people right after puberty. The devil pretty much knows the *spirit of lust* will drive men (and women) into sin and more sin.

Once they sin, the devil inserts whatever *spirits* he wants into their lives, and even into *them*. Now they are on either on a quick or a slow path to destruction because most if not all of their decisions and choices will be colored by lust, selfishness, and other works of the flesh.

The desire for other women is the *polygamy spirit*. Because what? You're so great there is no **one** person who is good enough to be with you, or can satisfy you?

If you were spiritually married from the womb and didn't even know it that is the *spirit of polygamy* acting in a bloodline.

Men are after me, women are after me, I don't know why I'm so desirable. Nope, not necessarily. It is more like the *spirit of polygamy* talking to other people's *spirit of polygamy* trying to tie you two together for the devil's purposes.

If you've got at least one baby momma or at least one baby daddy but you're not in a godly covenanted marriage with the other parent, that is the *spirit of polygamy* at work. Not as an out, but that spirit was loosed and acting full force on the American plantation when men were

made to stud service and women were forced to give birth to babies which were sold into more slavery.

Both then and now, offspring born because of or through this *polygamous spirit* are not safe in this Earth. Children of polygamous relationships are at the greatest risk of peril and captivity. That's only the start of what this spirit does to your kids.

Where envy and strife are, there is confusion and every evil work (James 3:16). Accidental pregnancy is more of the effects of the *spirit of polygamy.* Abject poverty, envy, strife. Here, I get the answer to my frequently asked question, *Why there are so many single mothers?* These women can't keep one partner, usually by no fault of their own. If the man or either of them have this *polygamous spirit* in their bloodline and they are not saved, not prayerful, not doing anything about it, they are at its mercy. But it has no mercy.

Threesomes, *menage trois*, freaky, perverse sex, wife for the night, husband for today only--, any evil thing that either party thinks up, desires or insists on is all from this *spirit of polygamy.* Lust can never be satisfied. Orgies-- this will **not** keep a man, if anything the reproach of it will drive him away or rack you with guilt so you leave the relationship. No work of the flesh will heal the *spirit of polygamy*; it feeds it. It makes it worse and embeds it deeper into a bloodline.

Too Many Wives

More than one grown woman in a house is too many. As we said earlier, this is where the attempts for control, domination or manipulation start. A woman wants to control the husband (Genesis); maybe she really wants him. Maybe she just doesn't want the other wife (wives) to have him. Maybe she wants to one-up the other(s) as Peninnah wanted to, over Hannah. *Really*, what else does she have to do; they had maids and servants, so the man was their focus. Isn't that the way he wants it?

This same competition starts if the man has a wife, or a side chick that the real wife finds out about.

When/if this man has other children, she will want her children to be his favorite --, what if they are not? An evil woman may set out to destroy the lives of the children by the other wife or wives. She may embark on witchcraft to become what she feels is the most successful in this marital derangement.

She may want satanic power which is costly. The cost is usually blood. Blood is gotten by ruining or taking a life. The devil will not be satisfied with one.

She may get into witchcraft for money-, to get money and more money from the man or whatever source she can.

FYI: You cannot put two women who do not like each other together and tell them to *work it out* and make friends. They are not children that you can convince or force to do what you want them to do. They may apologize to each other, but they may not mean it. These grown women, especially if one or more is a witch or even a blind witch will *fake* working it out and now the battles and war has gone underground. Underground is where the underworld is. Now, the problem is far worse.

What women won't do to get and keep a man! Man, do you have any idea? Or are you *flattered* by this? Men will do things too, but we may not get to that in this book.

Sister wives--, no, don't do it!

A fellow I knew some time ago said, if he had known how dumb his baby momma was, he would have stayed with her. He continued, *She believed everything I said.* He said this as a joke, but that's not how I heard. Polygamy is an egomaniac's dream!

Common results of the polygamy are broken homes. Poverty. High debt. High mortality, high death rate. ID Discovery moments--, it's all too much. Suicides. Stress. Weak family models. Runaways. Underdevelopment. Vagabond children. Sexually transmitted diseases, & spiritually transmitted *demons*. Adultery.

This is all chaos and confusion. Would you want to be a child in this mess?

How different is this with multiple baby mommas, or multiple marriages with multiple mothers, multiple fathers, and ½ sibs all over the place? Not much difference. No woman goes into a marriage thinking this will be the outcome, but how many men think it's a badge of honor to have a lot of women? Well, man, **every woman you have slept with is a wife. You are officially polygamous.**

Men, most of you have no ability to manage your own emotions – being an emotional cripple is what a friend of mine has called it. Women not only want relationship, security, physicality, they want friendship-, someone who will *hear* them and listen to them. If you can't handle your own emotions, how will you do it for someone else? If you can't do this for yourself, how will you do it for **multiple** women/wives? If you can't do this for yourself, how will you do it for *beaucoup* kids?

Ask God for deliverance.

What It Does to the Kids

Polygamy fosters unnatural and ungodly competition and extreme competition between the children of the adults involved. These kids can be pitted against one another. They also must compete for the father's love, which is little to none and not easy to get. I know God said, **Be fruitful and multiply** and the man with a **quiver full of kids is blessed**, but who has enough love to give to double digits numbers of children by multiple wives who may live in different houses, compounds, apartments, whether they know about each other, or not? Love, attention, encouragement and time become commodities. *Who* is paying the bills and taking care of these kids? Dad is out working or should be. Kids need mom, but they need more than mom, they need Dad also. Where is he? With wife #2 or #3's, or in the arms of a strange woman or side chick.

Resentment and bitterness are brewing in the spouses and the children. This is no different than dad being out in the streets cheating. That's what it feels like to those who don't get his attention when they want or need it. You end up with confused, unsuccessful children; that's called *unexplainable failure*. A lot of time because there are evil spiritual interferences in the lives of everyone in that house. If there is one family of the polygamous group that is fine and the rest of the families are jacked – well, you already know I'm suspicious.

Jealousy

Jealousy flares up. Human jealousy is the cause of a lot of evil in the Bible and out of the Bible. Cain was jealous of Abel. Cain killed Abel.

Sarah thought up Hagar having Ishmael, but nagged Abraham until he sent Hagar and Ishmael away. Another polygamy saga. Two grown women in a house who both think they have *authority*, does not work. It just doesn't.

Jacob and Esau—same mother and father had jealousy issues. Jacob stole Esau's star and birthright.

Jacob was tricked into marrying Leah before he married Rachel, the one he really wanted. But Jacob also had two concubines, side chicks, whatever you want to call them. Their clan was a potpourri of folks, too. Genesis 30:14 shows Leah and Rachel wheeling and dealing with the aphrodisiacal mandrakes to get Jacob to sleep with Leah that night because it was important to these women to have children and they were both barren at the time.

Peninnah was giving Hannah a very hard time for not having a son while they shared one husband, Elkanah (1 Sam1:2).

Joseph and his 10 older brothers were also of a polygamous clan. They were jealous of him and also of their father's relationship with Joseph's mother, who was actually their aunt. They faked Joseph's death and sold him into slavery.

Was Absalom jealous of David? Yes, children can be jealous of their parents, especially if dad is having all the fun, or what a child may see as fun. Parents can also be jealous of their children, not jealous over, but jealous *of*.

Now, when the children get jealous of the other children, it really gets bad. There was a man who wouldn't give his own children lunch money, even if they asked, but would give lunch money to the *neighbor's* children when he saw them on the way to school in the mornings. He didn't want his own children that he lived in the house with the see him do this, but they did. Don't you think this affected the children of his marriage? And the biggest question, why? **Whose** kids were the neighbor's kids? Was there some witchcraft going on there? Was that man a narcissist or *polygamous* in *spirit*?

Polygamous witchcraft easily springs from jealousy.

I'm not saying all women are witches, nor are all men. But there is something ungodly about the man who wants a harem. Can a woman acquire a stable of men? If there is even one thing ungodly about any person, the devil has a way *in*. The devil loves to sow confusion, disaster and defeat. Steal. Kill. Destroy. As far as the devil is concerned a jacked-up marriage, or no marriage, just a string of baby momma's is as good as having babies for Babylon.

He's An Altar

See how demonic? This man is either an altar or believes he is one. His demonics have invited and or allowed the devil to set up an altar in him, which makes him a warlock. So, he collects a bevy of woman and some or all of them are witches, even blind witches as they compete and excessively compete with one another. It's the Maury and the Springer show. Dude loves this attention while the women make fools of themselves fighting over him.

Now he marries or cohabitates with a witch, the children are natural born witches. If married, they are ONE. Goes into equals married—they are both witches now. So, the children grow up in this mess. It's mass and refried confusion.

People in these situations put others in bondage. If a person dies with the key to another's bondage, well, what do we do?

Declare warfare.

- Lord, show me the secret behind this problem.

The Lord will give you the keys that you need for your warfare. From the times of John the Baptist, the Kingdom of God suffereth violence and the violent take it by force.

The cheating boyfriend (or girlfriend) is horrendous and hurtful. Even if unnamed, it is the *spirit of the cheater,* or the *spirit of the liar*, or the *spirit of polygamy* at work. The cheated on should get a foreboding and run away from this person, unless they **know** God has changed them. Many will give lip service to keep the current connection going, but they are narcissists, collecting women, for example. They want that attention and worship. Period. See how demonic this is?

Undercover polygamy is a thing. It's the call of *lust, t*he *spirit of lust*. A person is not spending time with you, doesn't know anything about you, is not in a relationship with you, but they are coming around or calling for sex, sexting, getting their thrills from you. You have been broken down for parts. Do I need to say what *part(s)*?

Do you recall TV miniseries where entire extended families lived together in the compound, on the estate, or at the ranch? The women didn't get along. The men didn't get along. Communal living doesn't work, in the movies and on TV. Dynasty, Falcon Crest, the Carrington's...*drama*. We want to watch it, but we don't want to **live** it. Or do we? Some people love the drama, they use drama to get attention.

Reports of polygamous homes or clans usually involves celebration or the notoriety of the **father** of all these children. I've never heard it said that he fathered 12 doctors, 8 lawyers, 4 architects, 7 engineers a brain surgeon and a rocket scientist. Nope it is all about that old man and the celebration that his member worked at least 20 times on 4 or 5 different women. Has he stolen all of those kids' stars so he could live his life to suit himself? Even today in this country some parents mortgage their children while they are still children. They steal their social security numbers and put utility bills in their children's names. Before the child is even 18 he has jacked up credit. That's right up there with star and destiny stealing.

Polygamous clans, the perfect star-stealing set up.

We are not supposed to worshipping at strange altars, especially if they are people. God has instructed us to destroy strange and idol altars. But man, the two things that he seems to want so much, strange altars and witchcraft. These are exactly what God told us NOT to do.

But ye shall destroy their altars, break their images, and cut down their groves:

Exodus 34:13

He Shouldn't Be

Anyone who is asking for or demanding worship is an *altar*, but they are not supposed to be.

What is an altar? An **altar** is a table in a Christian Church where the communion bread and the wine are placed. An altar is a table or flat-topped block used as the focus for religious ritual especially for making sacrifices or offerings. It is a place where we worship God. We want to honor God we invite the Spirit of God into our lives for many reasons: for

Wisdom, comfort, Peace, security, prosperity, health and healing.

We make a sacrifice at an altar if we want to change our destiny or someone's destiny that we may be praying for. On an altar, we can make sacrifices for others as in the OT, Job made regular sacrifices for his children, just in case they sinned.

An altar is any place really in modern times where you worship. Worship is reverence to God. Worship is when we're attributing honor to God and we're giving homage to God, paying respects to Him. Worship is when you're speaking well of God *to God*. Worship means to bow down to God, to bow down to the King of kings. Worship is a form of adoration; we adore God when we worship with intention and regularity.

So, there are altars to God. These altars were built by God's specifications. God taught the people how to build the altar and also how to worship Him-- exactly what to do to worship Him. God promised that wherever you build an altar to Him, He will be in the midst.

The word, *altar* is from a Hebrew word that means, *to sacrifice*. It is a place of sacrifice that could be made of earth or stone. A Godly altar is usually placed someplace very conspicuous.

The first mention in the Bible is an altar made by Noah after he had landed the Ark, (Genesis 8:20). Noah built an altar unto the Lord, and he took of every clean beast and offered burnt offerings on the altar and the Lord smelled sweet savor.

What You Worship Affects Destiny

And the LORD smelled a sweet savour; and the LORD said in his heart, I will not again curse the ground any more for man's sake; for the imagination of man's heart *is* evil from his youth; neither will I again smite any more every thing living, as I have done. While the earth remaineth, seedtime and harvest, and cold and heat, and summer and winter, and day and night shall not cease. (Genesis 8:20)

Noah built an ark and then built this altar and placed the sacrifice on it and so God came down and was very pleased with it.

So, God changed the **destiny** of mankind by saying, He wouldn't flood all the Earth again as He had done. He promised, as long as the Earth remains there will be seedtime and harvest, that is, summer and winter and day and night shall not cease.

I believe the Bible but the sacrifice that Noah made on that altar concerned me because Noah had just put the animals on the ark two by two, where did he get these clean animals to sacrifice? In doing research, we found that Noah was on the ark between 364 and 370 days so some new animals could have come forward in that time.

Altars were erected by Abraham in Genesis 12:13. Abraham built an altar to God where God instructed Abraham exactly what to put on the altar and how to make offerings to God to be pleasing to God. Isaac built altars, Jacob built altars, so did Moses, and Saul (1 Samuel 14:35).

These altars had various names based on their placement of what was to be burned on them there was an Outer Altar, an Earthen Altar, Great Altar, Table of the Lord, there was and

Outdoor Altar in the court of the priest between the temple and the Court of Israel.

No where in the Bible did God ever instruct anyone to build an altar *from* a human or *to* a human. God even told the people to move on after 30 days when Moses died so they wouldn't worship dead Moses.

Different sacrifices were all offered on these altars, meat offerings, drink offerings, libations of wine were poured there. The sacrifices were to be seasoned with salt and this is all directed by God, but this was not a BBQ. This is an altar.

According to the Bible the fire on the altar was lit directly by the hand of God and this was not permitted to go out. This means there would be continuous offerings made to the **Lord**, night and day.

No strange fire could be placed on this altar, but in Leviticus 10:1, Nadab and Abihu, sons of Aaron each of them took either of them his censer and put fire therein and put incense thereon and offered strange fire unto the Lord. The OT rule was only the high priest could offer the burnt incense at the altar. Aaron was the first to serve in that office of high priest at the time NOT his children--, this is not child's play.

Worship to God lasts throughout the night because the burnt offerings would remain on the altar throughout the night before they could be removed. Most often they were totally consumed.

Jesus was as an offering in substitution for our sins. What other person would be willing to be totally consumed, sacrificed on the altar of the Cross? Offerings are to be blemish-free, perfect, so what other human *could* be an offering on the Cross? Not the robbers on either side of Jesus on that day at Calvary. Thank You, Lord.

In the Book of the Revelation, day after day and night after night the angels and beasts around the throne of God are saying, *Holy, Holy, Holy* is the Lord God the Almighty the one who always was who is who is still to come.

The Elders were around the Throne of God saying, You are worthy, O God, to receive glory honor and power. For you created all things that exist because You created what You pleased.

Worship is real, worship is lasting; it is not just a fly-by-night thing.

When the Israelites came out of Egypt, into the Wilderness they had a portable altar that was carried along with them. So could continue even when on the go, maybe especially when you're distressed or on the run. **We should always be worshipping God.**

God is very specific about His worship and about altars He even told the priest what they should wear. He told them exactly how to burn incense before the Lord.

When the Babylonians captured the Hebrews, their altar was taken away, so the Hebrew's altar **worship** was taken away.

People of God, when the enemy captures your worship to God, he's serious and you're seriously messed up. **Do not ever let anybody stop, change, steal, or divert your worship.**

Later, after the Israelites came back from the Babylonian captivity the altar was re-erected by Ezra and it had to be *renewed* because pagan rituals were performed through pagan burnings and pagan sacrifices. For this reason, some of the older stones of the altar, had to be replaced, refurbished, renewed and rededicated.

People who are not following after God, those people who were into idolatry and chasing after a little g *gods* ruined a holy altar by putting pagan sacrifices to their little *gods* on our God's altar, perverting the use of it. This was also strange fire in the nostrils of God.

This brings us to the crux of this book. What difference does it make you may ask what's burning on a piece of stone? When the stone is an altar and the sacrifice is holy, it makes all the difference in the world. It makes all the difference to your life. It makes all the difference in the lives of everyone in your **bloodline. Your worship, or lack thereof makes** all the difference in the success or failure of an entire people.

When the stone is an altar and the sacrifice is **not** a sweet-smelling savor to God, it is a difference of life and death. Nadab and

Abihu offered strange fire before the Lord, and *they* were consumed.

Christian churches have one feature in common, the altar. It is usually the communion table and is usually front and center, in a very conspicuous place, and it is set aside for God's use. Evil human agents have altars, most often they are hidden.

Conversely, the audacity of a man to erect *himself* as an altar and ask for or demand sacrifice should give us all pause.

An altar has serious significance, and its location is important. A person who declares *himself* an altar by words and/or actions is usually a sneaky sort. Well, unless he's a cult leader.

According to the Word, churches have also had to build that altar, and the position and the location of the table that represents the altar is very important.

The altar is where we invoke the Spirit of God. We invoke His presence and His angelic presence. Where the Spirit of God is there is liberty, and there are blessings.

We want **God** to change us, to change our lives to change our destinies to what **He** wants it to be especially if we stepped off of our path and have sinned and fallen short of the glory of God. Destinies can be changed at an altar.

At the altar, we are communing with God; we *invite* the presence of God.

Man is designed to worship; he will worship *something* and that's why we have to train up our children. Train up a child in the way they should go because if a person is not taught to worship God if he's not trained up in the faith and worship, or if he opts to rebel and not worship the Only Living God, he will worship *something*. He will either worship something he decides to worship on his own, or something that's set before him--, something that he's been told to worship. He might worship what his friends worship, and so on.

If he's been sold a bill of goods that's what he could worship. Maybe it's his truck, his house, his woman, his TV, his sports, his clothes, his watch collection, his jewelry, his weapons.

A woman may worship her handbag collection, her shoes, shopping. Maybe a person will worship their spouse, their children, their parents, their education, their degrees, their own success--, something. It's very common. How about this one? Money. A golden calf. Since we should be worshipping **God** at all times, we have to STOP doing that in order to worship an idol that we have either chosen or allowed to be chosen for us.

When worship to God stops and worship to any idol starts, another destiny changes. This time, not for good. Not at all. And, not smart.

Where your treasure is that's where your heart will be, also. So what you think on either 24/7 or most of the time, that's where you worship This is why God said not to worry because when you're putting your mind on a thing, or on a person, that's a form of worship.

Even if you're not sending them hearts and flowers and happiness-- even if it's a worry, or the pain from a jilted soul tie, then you are at the altar of that *person* to worship them, in a sense.

Even if it's to the negative because of all the stuff that they have done to you, you it's still worship because they're occupying a place in your mind. So, whether you know it or not this person is occupying the space in your head, dominating your thoughts, controlling your time, and they are *manipulating* the situation, or they may be manipulating **you.**

Should continue doing this or should you make changes? You have to pray to God!

When the altar is changed a person's destiny is changed. When the offerings change, a person's destiny is changed. When the worship style, frequency is changed, destiny changes. Most importantly when the *object* of the worship changes, destiny is changed.

The destiny of how many people, how many women and children are changed because they worshipped at the altar of a polygamist? He's the altar. You worship what you worship. There is nothing left for anyone else, at least nothing pure.

You lose yourself; you lose. You are the sacrifice at his altar. You've sold yourself, and for what?

Only Jesus can buy you back; else, your destiny is lost, or sold if you did it knowingly.

In time, and with discernment, you may find that the polygamist that you worship is a big deal to the devil, after all, who put that altar in him? At death he will go to hell. You worship him, so you will have to go there too. Your worship determines your destiny. Or are you planning at the last minute like the malefactor on the cross beside Jesus to *repent*? One on either side of Jesus accepted Him and one did not. Which one will you be?

How will you know when the last minute *is*?

Repent now.

The Narcissist

An altar is wherever you worship and perhaps in this worship you've brought items to the worship. Perhaps you *haven't* perhaps **_you_** are what you brought to the worship. Yeah, I will mention narcissism. Perhaps you are enchanted by your looks, your hair, your skin, your face, your physique, your curves, your thinness, your muscles, your smartness, your voice, your other gifts your talents--, well we know you got any and all of this stuff from God but *you're giving yourself credit for* it.

There was a beautiful angel named Lucifer. Gifted, yes. Beautiful, yes. Talented, yes. Smart, probably. He was at least tricky.

When a person decides that they have <u>made</u> themselves, and that they are awesome, they are worshipping *themselves*. If you decide that you pulled yourself up by your own bootstraps, are you going to worship your boots? Are you going to worship your bootstraps? No.

You should be worshipping God because He made you, gave you the smarts. He gave you the wherewithal, He gave you the opportunities to bring yourself up from where you were to a destiny or future that He had promised you.

Instead of praising God a narcissist praises himself for his accomplishments giving themselves all the pats on back, and all the credit. Their altar is their bathroom mirror--, any mirror really, and the altar table is their bathroom counter with all those jams and jellies, makeup, and skin care products.

I'm not saying you shouldn't look your best at all times, but self-worship is too much it's not of God.

We are to worship God. We are to love the Lord our God with all our hearts all our souls, all of our mind and with all of our strength.

You can find out if a person is a narcissist and if they worship themselves or not. Just *listen* to what they talk about the most; that's what they worship. Even if you ask this person what they believe in or where they go to church, or even *if* they go to church if they refuse to talk *about* God that's a strong clue. Let them talk and they would eventually tell you about the thing or the things that they worship.

In the Old Testament Book of Esther Mordecai, Esther's uncle refused to bow to Haman. Haman was infuriated by this because he wanted attention, he wanted recognition all the time. Haman was a narcissist--, it doesn't say it that way in the Bible, but he was perfect example of a raging narcissist.

Later on in the chapter it talks about how the king was putting on a banquet to honor someone. Haman immediately thought that the banquet must be for him and that's when he said, *"Who better to honor than me?"* This is typical conversation for a narcissist.

In your interpersonal relationships if you've **never** dated a narcissist, you may *be* the narcissist.

Sorry.

A narcissistic person has an inflated sense of importance. They have a **deep** need for constant attention, excessive admiration and control. They have a past and probably future riddled with messed up, toxic relationships because they don't have any empathy for anybody else, only themselves. They're the only important person, your feelings are not important. It's all about them.

You didn't create yourself so you can't worship your ability to create people and especially not yourself. If you worship something that should not be worshipped, you will end up destroying it and yourself along with it. If the thing you worship is yourself--, you will have destroyed yourself.

Even though the narcissist is a lover of self, that's not enough. He wants more adoration, so he tries to get other people to worship him.

There was a beautiful angel named Lucifer; he wanted and still wants worship, so he is still trying to get people to worship him. Lucifer fell from Heaven and a third of the stars--, that's a third of the angels fell with him. A third of them were willing to worship the devil. Self-worship is not gratifying because no amount of worship is enough.

We are trying to win souls so they won't go to hell while the devil is trying to buy, trick, trap people into worshipping him so they *will* go to hell.

No one can really legally worship any other than God; that's idolatry and in the end, it will destroy both the idol and the idolater. Once the idolater is destroyed, that is as good as a blood sacrifice. We are talking about altars here, and what goes on an altar, but a sacrifice?

The narcissist has a litany, a list of toxic, troubled relationships following in their wake. They probably have the same for their future if they don't change. They don't care if they destroyed a person or destroyed a person's destiny, as long as they got what *they* wanted out of the transaction. Still, whatever they got, was not enough, because it is never enough.

They could have destroyed another emotionally, mentally, scholastically—they could have gaslit them, breadcrumbed them, lied to them --, done anything to them to keep them at their feet and under subjection. They will take worship even if it means tricking, intimidating, manipulating, controlling, dominating—any form of witchcraft-- a person into worship. For example, Mordecai didn't bow to Haman because emblazoned on Haman's garment was the image of an idol *god* and Mordecai refused to bow to that idol *god*. Mordecai was not tricked.

Once set up, the "altar" wants worship. When the worship is over from a particular source, they go look for another one because surely the person that was worshipping them must be flawed and must be something wrong with that person. There can't be anything wrong with the narcissist-- like *ever*.

When the evil altar, which takes on a life of its own DEMANDS another or a ***different*** sacrifice, the person enslaved by that altar must go get what the altar wants. This is why some people, men especially jump from woman to woman, relationship to relationship when nothing is wrong with the girl he's dating or married to. He is remote controlled by the power of that altar and the altar is directing him.

So, they go get another person and groom them and train them. These worshippers are *supply* to a narcissist and his altar. After this one they will get another and then another, and so on to get the worship they deeply desire and feel they deserve.

In this way, the narcissist makes himself or herself the **altar** because the devil has set up an altar inside that person.

Any worship at an evil altar is idolatrous strange fire because it is not to God. The narcissist has a grandiose sense of self-importance, he is preoccupied with fantasies of his wonderfulness of his unlimited success, power, brilliance, beauty, or swag. He feels he is super special, unique, and wonders if anyone else even gets how amazing he is. He may wonder if anybody can understand his vast intelligence and brilliance, but he knows that he just can't just deal with just anybody and so, he only deals with elite people, those of high status and celebrity. But it is his altar that's telling him all this.

No matter what he gets or how much, it is never enough. I believe these people have a deep dark hole in their souls that can never be filled, unless they let Jesus heal them. He needs deliverance. The narcissist has a sense of entitlement, and they will exploit people, easily. They don't care they just want what they want. They will take anything from anybody at any time. They don't care. They are takers mostly, rarely givers, and only to groom a *supply*. They aren't usually in relationships with people, they are making transactions with people, although they may have you thinking it's a relationship.

They have no empathy they are the only important person in the world. They really believe they are the center of the world, and everyone should revolve around them adore them, worship them, notice them, and give them things.

They are envious and jealous of other people. These people make horrible spouses, horrible parents, horrible siblings. Even if they weren't raised by polygamous people/polygamous families, they behave classically as if they were.

A narcissist needs to be saved and submit to the Holy Spirit, else his behavior, attitudes and actions will damage and could destroy himself and everyone in his environment.

God gives Grace, Mercy and in that is time to see the error of one's ways and change. Even though He gives Grace, many times, the sooner one comes under conviction and changes, the better. After death, there are no do overs.

If God reprimands you or convicts you of sin sooner than later that means He wants you to get it right, come to Him and repent so he won't have to *judge* you.

Numbers 25:27 says, it is not good to eat much honey and men who speak of their own glory is not glory at all. The narcissist makes himself the altar, and those who come to worship him, are the **sacrifice**. When your life is not worshipping God and is instead worshipping an idol, where is your *life*, really?

This is a strong perversion of and diversion from what God intended when He told men to make an altar and told them exactly how to worship.

Worship

Remember you are to love the Lord our God with all your heart with all your soul, mind, and strength, Mark 12:30.

Read this aloud:

Let God arise, let his enemies be scattered: let them also that hate him flee before him.

As smoke is driven away, so drive them away: as wax melteth before the fire, so let the wicked perish at the presence of God.

But let the righteous be glad; let them rejoice before God: yea, let them exceedingly rejoice.

Sing unto God, sing praises to his name: extol him that rideth upon the heavens by his name JAH, and rejoice before him.

A father of the fatherless, and a judge of the widows, is God in his holy habitation.

God setteth the solitary in families: he bringeth out those which are bound with chains: but the rebellious dwell in a dry land.

O God, when thou wentest forth before thy people, when thou didst march through the wilderness; Selah:

The earth shook, the heavens also dropped at the presence of God: even Sinai itself was moved at the presence of God, the God of Israel.

Thou, O God, didst send a plentiful rain, whereby thou didst confirm thine inheritance, when it was weary.

Thy congregation hath dwelt therein: thou, O God, hast prepared of thy goodness for the poor.

The Lord gave the word: great was the company of those that published it.

[12] Kings of armies did flee apace: and she that
tarried at home divided the spoil.

Though ye have lien among the pots yet shall
ye be as the wings of a dove covered with
silver, and her feathers with yellow gold.

When the Almighty scattered kings in it, it
was white as snow in Salmon.

The hill of God is as the hill of Bashan; an
high hill as the hill of Bashan.

Why leap ye, ye high hills? this is the hill
which God desireth to dwell in; yea,
the LORD will dwell in it for ever.

The chariots of God are twenty thousand, even
thousands of angels: the Lord is among them,
as in Sinai, in the holy place.

Thou hast ascended on high, thou hast led
captivity captive: thou hast received gifts for
men; yea, for the rebellious also, that
the LORD God might dwell among them.

Blessed be the Lord, who daily loadeth us with
benefits, even the God of our salvation. Selah.

He that is our God is the God of salvation; and
unto GOD the Lord belong the issues from
death.

But God shall wound the head of his enemies,
and the hairy scalp of such an one as goeth on
still in his trespasses.

The Lord said, I will bring again from Bashan,
I will bring my people again from the depths
of the sea:

That thy foot may be dipped in the blood of
thine enemies, and the tongue of thy dogs in
the same.

They have seen thy goings, O God; even the
goings of my God, my King, in the sanctuary.

The singers went before, the players on
instruments followed after; among them were
the damsels playing with timbrels.

Bless ye God in the congregations, even the
Lord, from the fountain of Israel.

There is little Benjamin with their ruler, the
princes of Judah and their council, the princes
of Zebulun, and the princes of Naphtali.

Thy God hath commanded thy strength: strengthen, O God, that which thou hast wrought for us.

Because of thy temple at Jerusalem shall kings bring presents unto thee.

[30] Rebuke the company of spearmen, the multitude of the bulls, with the calves of the people, till every one submit himself with pieces of silver: scatter thou the people that delight in war.

Princes shall come out of Egypt; Ethiopia shall soon stretch out her hands unto God.

Sing unto God, ye kingdoms of the earth; O sing praises unto the Lord; Selah:

To him that rideth upon the heavens of heavens, which were of old; lo, he doth send out his voice, and that a mighty voice.

Ascribe ye strength unto God: his excellency is over Israel, and his strength is in the clouds.

O God, thou art terrible out of thy holy places: the God of Israel is he that giveth strength and power unto his people. Blessed be God.

That was Psalm 68 and that was worship to God. That was not too long; that was worship--, blessed be God.

We worship the Lord; **He** can be an Altar, but no one else. God hates idolatry.

Spiritual Polygamy

How many *gods* do you think you can have, serve, or be in *covenant* with? How many can you be in relationship with on a daily basis?

How many "spouses" can you conduct a *relationship* with? The question is not how many you want to have sex with. Lust of the eye, lust of the flesh, pride of life – lust is never satisfied, until you bring it under control.

Goes into equals **married** and it is a **covenant.** How much fun can it be to know that the person you are in covenant with is **violating** your covenant in the bedroom of another woman that he is violating?

If you were stirring up a cake batter and ate off the spoon, I don't want that spoon; I will not taste the batter after you, so don't put it back into the cake bowl, either. What are we talking about here? This is nasty.

The violation of covenant is a terrible thing; the physical act is right there in your face, and that's even worse. That's the beginning of the jealousy, resentment, hatred, confusion and the evil.

People say you will treat your boyfriend/girlfriend/spouse exactly the way you treat God. God hates polygamy. He is Jealous, spiritually speaking. Further, God does not want you parceling yourself out, fragmenting your soul and spirit, chasing after idol *gods*, or men who have promoted themselves as false Christs or something to be adored.

The Lord, Our God is **ONE** and Jesus made people WHOLE. There are lessons in all of that.

God is JEALOUS. Yeah, that's one of His names, **JEALOUS**.

Like me, you also may have thought that none of this has anything to do with you. It very well could. It probably--, definitely could.

In the Bible, goes into equals married. Yes, **you have married <u>everyone</u> you've ever had sex with**, whether consensual or not.

Sorry.

In the Bible when men were tired of women, they had the option to *put them away*; that is leave them or send them away without a proper divorce. This was especially doable if they were never officially married in the first place--, you know shacking up, living together, or cohabitating.

So, unless you have officially and properly divorced <u>every</u> person you've ever slept with, **you are polygamous**, and a *polygamous spirit* resides with you. It distracts you; it takes your time, it messes with your head and makes you ask, what ifs, and wonder if a certain one got away. It makes you constantly look for other *options* and relationship upgrades. In this way it pulls your whole heart from your Earth spouse and marriage. It pulls your heart from your real kids. It leads you into soul ties. It wastes time and spends your money, chasing flesh.

If you have baby momma's, baby daddies, and kids in more than one household, Ex's all over the place, that is also a *polygamous spirit* in operation. It is one of the reasons why children with only one parent in the home must surmount incredible odds to do even normal things and have normal success. The *polygamous spirit* in the home deprives a child of so much, and wounds him, sometimes for life.

Even if you are perfect, your daddy's polygamous ways have affected you spiritually and naturally. Your momma's ways have affected you spiritually and in the natural--, and so on down your ancestral line. Do you see how this compounds, adds, even multiplies exponentially so the demon of polygamy is in your family as a stronghold?

The well-meaning relative or parent who said, *Don't marry the first one, date around.*

The dad who told his son to sow wild oats was probably only repeating what had been said to him and did not know the spiritual damage he was setting his child and his grandchildren up for.

Guard Yourself

We must guard ourselves, have the Mind of Christ and soul prosperity, using Wisdom. The Church as a collective whole is to be married to Jesus Christ, the Bridegroom. We cannot be jealous of one another. There is enough **God** to go around. He is Omnipresent. He is Omniscient. He is Omnipotent; no human being is all that.

There is nothing lacking, nothing missing or broken in Him. God gives gifts severally and as He will. Some saints of God are jealous of gifts, they are jealous of titles, callings, abilities, anointing, … this human jealousy is a work of the flesh, and it is NOT of God.

There are no perfect people. There are no perfect husbands, except One, and if we all and each get to be married collectively to that one, as long as we are ONE, united, then it is ONE church married to ONE bridegroom, and Amen.

Repent of your own sins.

Repent for your ancestors' sins back to Adam & Eve.

Break covenants.

Break curses.

Break bondages and yokes.

- All my virtues stolen by polygamous witchcraft, be released now, by fire, in Jesus' Name.
- Polygamous covering hiding my star catch fire, in Jesus' Name.

There are about 40 instances of polygamy in the Bible and they each reap bitterness. If you're a cheater, you can't think that just because "they" don't know it won't hurt them. Life is spiritual. Spiritual things will *find* you.

Typical bondage from growing up in a polygamist home includes that you will find that you are also a cheater. Cheaters can't just date one person. Evil exchange/transference of virtues happens in polygamous homes. Female oppression, teen pregnancy, rape, premature death, prostitution, weak family units, illegitimate children.

Curses are enchanted and programmed against the children, ruthlessly by the multiple wives.

- Bondages programmed into my life by any dead person, die in Jesus' Name.
- Every curse issued against me while I was in the womb, DIE! in Jesus' Name.
- Every battle programmed into my life by polygamous witchcraft, I dislodge, break, and dismantle your curse against me. I break your satanic clock, calendar, and counterfeit scroll. I break your connection with any Triangular Power against me. Back to sender.
- Evil power, you will not capture my head. Any arrow fired into the head, the Lord render it harmless to me, return to sender, in the Name of Jesus.

Warfare Prayers

I repent of all sins, known sins, unknown sins. Sins of omission and commission, in the Name of Jesus. I repent of the sins of my ancestors, especially sins of lust, rolling stones, *whoredoms*, promiscuity, perversion, any sexual sins including sins of **polygamy**, in the Name of Jesus.

Lord, cover me with the Blood of Jesus. I don't know the sins my ancestors committed. I don't even know all the sins I have committed, in the dream. Lord, forgive every sin, in the Name of Jesus.

Mercy!

Lord, pour Your salt into my foundation and heal it, in Jesus' Name.

Lord, let every evil imagination against me wither away from the root, in the Name of Jesus. I shall overcome by the Blood of the Lamb and the Word of my testimony, in the Name of Jesus.

Let every plan for my downgade or destruction blow up in the enemy's face, in the Name of Jesus.

All powers advocating evil plans against me, be disgraced, in the Name of Jesus.

All stubborn, evil strongman delegated against me, fall down and become impotent, in the Name of Jesus.

I withdraw my husband's attention from the strange woman, in the Name of Jesus.

I bind the spirit of desiring to be worshipped off my spouse, in the Name of Jesus.

I bind the spirit of unsanctioned, ungodly rescue of strange women with evil agendas, in the Name of Jesus.

I stand against every power of polygamy, in the Name of Jesus.

I break every evil covenant in my bloodline and in my husband's bloodline, involving polygamy in any and all of its forms, in the Name of Jesus.

All spiritual evil arrows fired from the strange woman sent into my husband or marriage or against my children, lose your power and every evil network connection, in the Name of Jesus.

I *loose* the power for that strange woman to get her own husband, that is not my husband

and to live happily ever after, in the Name of Jesus.

Let confusion be the lot for every strange woman coming against my marriage.

Lord, put a sword between my husband and the strange woman, in the Name of Jesus.

Angel of God, pursue, discomfit and disconnect the relationship between my husband and the strange woman, whether it be emotional or physical or any other type of ungodly relationship, in Jesus's Name.

I cry Mercy for myself, my children and my husband, Lord, and I call judgment on every unrelenting pursuer of my spouse, in the Name of Jesus.

I nullify every evil judgment that is against me and my marriage, in the Name of Jesus.

Thank You, Lord.

I break every bondage against me, my family, my marriage, in the Name of Jesus. I break every covenant and curse that allows the bondage to stand. I permanently dismiss every evil demon connected to this bondage or in place to enforce this bondage in my life. Back to sender, in the Name of Jesus.

Lord, deliver me from every inherited curse, hex, vex, incantation, enchantment, charm, sorcery, hoodoo, voodoo, black magic, red magic, white magic, green magic, in the Name of Jesus.

Lord, set your Fire Axe to the foundation of my life; destroy every evil plantation.

Let the Blood of Jesus flush out from my system every inherited satanic deposit, in the Name of Jesus. I release myself from the grip of any problem transferred into my life, from my inception, in the Name of Jesus.

Let the Blood of Jesus and the fire of the Holy Ghost cleanse every organ in my body, in the Name of Jesus.

I vomit every evil consumption, both from the natural and in the spirit/dream that I have been fed from childhood up until now, in the Name of Jesus.

Lord, break every evil effect of every evil hand that has ever held me, babysat me, played with me, fed me, or touched me, in the Name of Jesus.

I command all foundational strong men, evil strong men attached to my life, to be bound and then paralyzed, in Jesus' Name.   Lord, render every organized strategy of the devil's camp against my life, useless, in the Name of Jesus.

I command all demonic spirits transferred into my life through evil touch or the evil laying on of hands to be negated and cast into the fire, in the Name of Jesus.

Lord, let every demonic influence targeted at destroying my spiritual vision, dream, and ministry fail totally, in Jesus' Name.

Lord, give me victory over secret curses, in the Name of Jesus.

Lord, reveal to me everything I need to know about this attack, this battle and the enemy's plans against me, in the Name of Jesus.

I command all curses issued against me to be broken, in the Name of Jesus. I command all evil spirits associated with any curse to leave me now, return to sender, in the Name of Jesus and know that Jesus is Lord.

Lord, shield me from every evil arrow, manipulation, and attack in all areas of my life, in the Name of Jesus.

Lord, shield my children from every evil arrow, manipulation, loss of virtue, and evil exchange in all areas of their lives, in the Name of Jesus.

I reject every deceptive family member and all household witchcraft, in the Name of Jesus.

Let the curse of impossibility issued against me return to the enemy 7-fold, in the Name of Jesus.

Let every evil agent of impossibility fashioned against me, receive punishment according to the evil in their hearts, in the Name of Jesus.

I declare and decree that every plantation of impossibility in my life is uprooted, withers and dies, in the Name of Jesus.

Lord, send Your axe of fire to the foundation of my life and destroy every evil plantation at its root, in the Name of Jesus.

My life, receive fire, become fire, in Jesus' Name. (at least 7 times)

Lord, let the Blood of Jesus flush out of my system every inherited satanic deposit, in the Name of Jesus.

I break and loose myself from every collective evil family covenant, in the Name of Jesus.

I break loose from every collective family curse, in the Name of Jesus, Amen.

All evil networks against me, I break your connection now, and I send confusion into your camps, in the Name of Jesus.

I command all demonic mirrors and monitoring gadgets against my life to crack, fall way, melt to pieces, in the Name of Jesus.

Lightning and Thunder of God break up every evil altar whether household, environmental, or territorial, whether individual or of a coven, whether manual or automatic, in the Name of Jesus.

I command every agent of poverty to lose *its hold over my life, in the Name of Jesus. Spirit of poverty* lose your grip over my life; Power of Wealth and Blood of Jesus speak for me, work for me in the Name of Jesus.

I bind the *spirit of disappointment* and almost there, in the Name of Jesus.

I command every agent of debt to lose its hold over my life; Blood of Jesus answer for me, in the Name of Jesus.

Lord, let every problem connected to polygamy in my life be nullified by the power of Jesus Christ.

Every power of any family idol whether an object, idea, or person that is affecting my life, my home and my work, be broken now, in the Name of Jesus.

I command every satanic reinforcement against me to scatter to smitherings, in the Name of Jesus.

I cancel all evil vows and sacrifices that are affecting me negatively now, in the Name of Jesus.

Lord, let the clock and the timetable of the enemy regarding my life be destroyed and never put back together against me again, in the Name of Jesus.

I bind the *spirits of retribution,* retaliation, and payback because of these prayers, in the Name of Jesus.

I seal these declarations across every timeline, dimension, realm, age, past present and future to infinity, and across every dimension, in the Name of Jesus.

AMEN.

Other books by this author

AK: The Adventures of the Agape Kid

Already Married in the Spirit: *Why You May Not Be Married in the Natural*

AMONG SOME THIEVES

Ancestral Powers

Anti-Marriage, *The Spirit of*

Backstabbers https://a.co/d/gi8iBxf

Barrenness, *Prayers Against* https://a.co/d/feUltIs

Battlefield of Marriage, *The*

Beware of the Dog: Prayers Against Dogs in the Dream.

Bless Your Food: *Let the Dining Table be Undefiled*

Blindsided: *Has the Old Man Bewitched You?* https://a.co/d/5O2fLLR

Break Free from Collective Captivity

Broken Spirits & Dry Bones

Casting Down Imaginations

Churchzilla, The Wanna-Be, Supposed-to-be Bride of Christ

Demonic Cobwebs (prayerbook)

Demonic Time Bombs

Demons Hate Questions

Devil Loves Trauma, *The*

Devil Weapons: Unforgiveness, Bitterness,…

The Devourers: Thieves of Darkness 2

Do Not Swear by the Moon

Don't Refuse Me, Lord (4 book series)
https://a.co/d/idP34LG

Dream Defilement

The Emptiers: *Thieves of Darkness, 1*
https://a.co/d/5I4n5mc

Evil Touch

Failed Assignment

Fantasy Spirit Spouse https://a.co/d/hW7oYbX

FAT Demons (The): *Breaking Demonic Curses*
https://a.co/d/4kP8wV1

The Fold (5-book series)

- The Fold (Book 1)
- Name Your Seed (Book 2)
- The Poor Attitudes of Money (3)
- Do Not Orphan Your Seed (4)
- For the Sake of the Gospel (5)
- My Sowing Journal

Gang Ups: Touch Not God's Anointed

Getting Rid of Evil Spiritual Food

https://a.co/d/i2L3WYQ

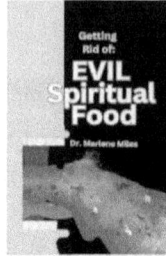

got HEALING? Verses for Life

got LOVE? Verses for Life

got HOPE? Verses for Life

got money? https://a.co/d/g2av41N

How to Dental Assist

How to Dental Assist2: Be Productive, Not Wasteful

How to STOP Being a Blind Witch or Warlock

I Take It Back

Legacy

Let Me Have A Dollar's Worth https://a.co/d/h8F8XgE

Level the Playing Field

Living for the NOW of God

Lose My Location https://a.co/d/crD6mV9

Love Breaks Your Heart

Made Perfect In Love

Man Safari, *The*

Marriage Ed. Rules of Engagement & Marriage

Made Perfect in Love

Money Hunters: Beware of Those

Money on the Altar https://a.co/d/4EqJ2Nr

Mulberry Tree, *The* https://a.co/d/9nR9rRb

Motherboard (The) - *Soul Prosperity Series*

Name Your Seed

Occupy: *Until I Return*

Plantation Souls

Players Gonna Play

Power Money: Nine Times the Tithe https://a.co/d/gRt41gy

The Power of Wealth *(forthcoming)*

Powers Above

The Robe, Part 1, The Lessons of Joseph

The Robe, Part II, The Lessons of Joseph

Seasons of Grief

Seasons of Waiting

Seasons of War

Second Marriage, Third--, *Any Marriage*
https://a.co/d/6m6GN4N

Sift You Like Wheat

Six Men Short: What Has Happened to all the Men?

Soul Prosperity soul prosperity series 3

https://a.co/d/5p8YvCN

Souls Captivity soul prosperity series 2

The Spirit of Anti-Marriage

The Spirit of Poverty

StarStruck

SUNBLOCK

The Swallowers: *Thieves of Darkness*, 3

Take It Back

This Is NOT That: How to Keep Demons from Coming at You

Time Is of the Essence

Too Many Wives: *Why You Have Lady Problems*

Tormenting Spirits   https://a.co/d/dAogEJf

Toxic Souls

Triangular Power *(series)*

- Powers Above
- SUNBLOCK
- Do Not Swear by the Moon
- STARSTRUCK

Unbreak My Heart: *Don't Let Me Die*

Uncontested Doom

Unguarded Hours, *The*

Unseen Life, *The* (forthcoming)

Upgrade: How to Get Out of Survival Mode

- Toxic Souls (Book 2 of series)
- Legacy (Book 3 of series)

The Wasters: *Thieves of Darkness,* Bk 2
https://a.co/d/bUvl9Jo

What Have You to Declare? What Do You Have With You from Where You've Been?

When I Was A Child, *I Prayed As a Child*

When the Devourer is Rebuked

https://a.co/d/1HVv8oq

The Wilderness Romance *(series)* This series is about conducting a Godly relationship and marriage with someone who is a Wilderness person. It is about how to recognize it and navigate through it. These books are about how not to get caught up in such.

- *The Social Wilderness*
- *The Sexual Wilderness*
- *The Spiritual Wilderness*

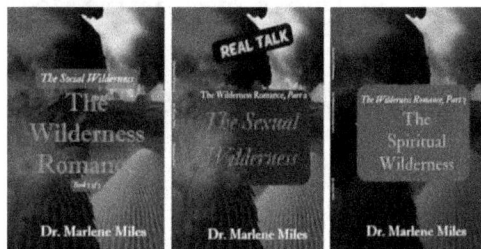

Other Series

The Fold (a series on Godly finances) https://a.co/d/4hz3unj

Soul Prosperity Series https://a.co/d/bz2M42q

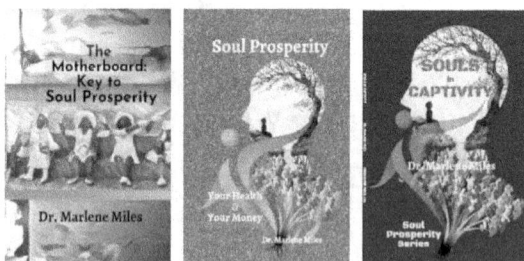

Spirit Spouse books

https://a.co/d/9VehDSo

https://a.co/d/97sKOwm

Battlefield of Marriage, The

https://a.co/d/eUDzizO

Players Gonna Play

https://a.co/d/2hzGw3N

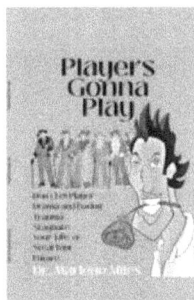

Matters of the Heart

Made Perfect in Love https://a.co/d/70MQW3O

Love Breaks Your Heart https://a.co/d/4KvuQLZ

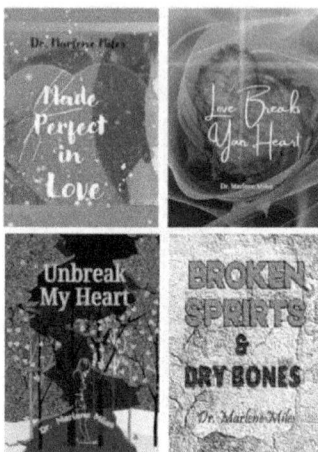

Unbreak My Heart https://a.co/d/84ceZ6M

Broken Spirits & Dry Bones https://a.co/d/e6iedNP

Thieves of Darkness series

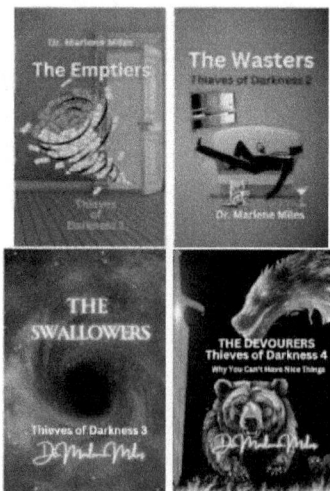

The Emptiers https://a.co/d/heio0dO

The Wasters https://a.co/d/5TG1iNQ

The Swallowers https://a.co/d/1jWhM6G

The Devourers: Why We Can't Have Nice Things
https://a.co/d/87Tejbf

Triangular Powers https://a.co/d/aUCjAWC

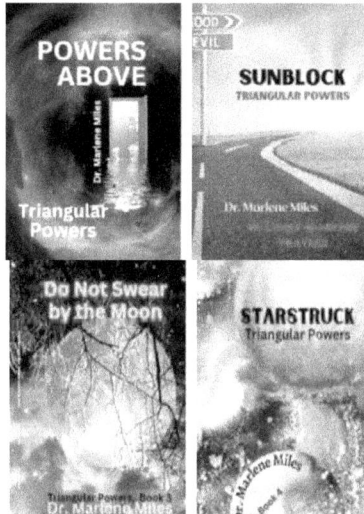

Upgrade (series) *How to Get Out of Survival Mode*
https://a.co/d/aTERhX0